Mull & Iona

Mull & Iona

By

Allan Wright

First Published in Great Britain by

Lyrical Scotland an imprint of Cauldron Press Ltd
Parton House Stables
Castle Douglas
Kirkcudbrightshire
Scotland
DG7 3NB

www.lyricalscotland.com

ISBN10: 0-9551143-2-2
ISBN13: 978-0-9551143-2-8

British Library Cataloguing-in-Publication Data
A catalogue record for this book is available on request from the British Library

Jacket design by Isobel Bathgate
Layout and captions by Allan Wright
Page make up by Small Print Castle Douglas
Printed in Poland

Preface

The islands of Mull and Iona are bountiful and very special places. If, like me, you are easily impressed, you will find yourself overwhelmed by their scale and rendered breathless by their beauty. I hope the images in this book will serve to intensify the experience of these islands for anyone who has or will set foot here.

I had some short but intense travel experiences of Mull and Iona during the 1980s and 90s, but it was in 2002 that I began a more comprehensive island odyssey. I chose these islands as my starting point, thinking that a week or so would generate enough material. However, I soon realised that I had seriously underestimated the attraction these islands would hold for me. The more I explored the landscape and unique atmosphere, the stronger the compulsion I felt to return and try to do justice to the place. I found it hard to draw a line under it in order to complete this project as I was fully aware that there was more to do. But then, as wise people will tell you, it is best to leave the table slightly hungry.

People often ask me: How long did you have to wait to get that particular picture? The answer is not a trade secret, as it is usually the case that the shot was more or less immediate. It happened because I was there at the right time, and there are thousands of right times happening all over the place at any given moment. Harvest time comes when you are out there moving and being receptive. Places like the Hebrides are so dynamic in terms of light and colour that if you put in the miles – whether by car, cycle or foot – the essence of the landscape will reveal itself to you. And that is a promise.

I am no geologist, historian, or geographer. The story these pictures tell has the most elementary of structures: it progresses anti-clockwise from the ferry. The journey begins at the passing of the Lismore Lighthouse, which is not even on Mull. But the sight of it is so much a part of the experience that it has to be included. From Craignure we travel North through Salen to Tobermory then on to Glengorm, Dervaig and Calgary. We then move down the West Coast and round Loch Na Keal to Gribun before heading over to the Ross of Mull, out to Iona and back along the South Ross via Loch Buie. Our journey ends at Duart and Torosay.

I would like to dedicate the book to Martyn Bennet, one of Scotland's most brilliant musicians, who died on Mull in 2005. His music profoundly nourished my spirit as I explored these islands and I, like many others, was deeply shocked and moved by his untimely death. Martyn spent his latter years on Mull and is buried at Calgary.

Allan Wright

February 2006

Introduction

When the Mull Bard, Dugald MacPhail, wrote the chorus of his famous Gaelic song, he described the island of his birth in four lines that will suffice for our starting point.

An t-Eilean Muileach

An t-Eilean Muileach, an t-eilean aghmhar,
An t-eilean grianach mu'n iath an saile,
Eilean buadhmhor nam fuar-bheann arda,
Nan coilltean uaine, s' nan cluaintean fhasail.
Isle of Mull, pleasant island,
Sunny island surrounded by sea,
Glorious with its high cold hills,
Green woodlands and lonely pastures.

Despite the many changes since these lines were written, the island has retained its charm. When the sun shines it softens the landscape, the clarity of the air enhances the colours and one can almost taste the sweet air. When the dark clouds roll in the scenery can become moody and magnificent.

Most of Mull was born of fire. A large volcano situated in the region of Loch Ba sent lava flows far and wide. One geologist described Mull as looking like a wedding cake due to the stepped hills, formed by the erosion of the successive lava flows. The black volcanic rock is basalt which is very hard and fine-grained. Several important geological features are to be found, particularly the Fossil Tree at Ardmeanach, the Arches at Carsaig and the fascinating shorelines traversed to reach these wonderful places. As you progress along the Ross of Mull towards Iona, you become aware of a change of rock to red granite, a stone that was in great demand for important buildings throughout the United

Kingdom in Victorian times. On the south shore near Carsaig we find mudstone rich in fossils of a marine type such as Ammonites, Gryphea (Devil's Toe Nails) and Belemnites.

At the time when humans first arrived in the form of the hunter/gatherer tribes of the Mesolithic period 6,000 years ago, the island was approaching its climatic optimum. Food would have been plentiful, particularly around the sheltered bays. The Neolithic people came to the island around 4,500BC. They were the first farmers. They had domesticated animals and cultivated the land. They buried their dead communally in chambered tombs. It is believed that they were a peaceful people. The next arrivals, in the Third Millennium BC, were the people of the Bronze Age. It was they who erected the stone circle at Lochbuie and the many standing stones on the island. They buried their dead singly in round cairns surrounded by large kerb stones. It was during this period in the island's history that a rapid deterioration in the climate occurred. It became much wetter, and peat began to accumulate. Around 500 BC the Celtic people started to arrive. They appear to have been very territorial, as a large number of Forts and Duns were constructed around the island, along with two ruinous Brochs. A visit to one or more of the prehistoric sites is a must.

In AD703 St Adamnan, Abbot of Iona, wrote in his 'Life of St Columba' of the arrival on Iona of the saint in AD563 and his subsequent conversion of the Picts of the east. He also wrote about the attacks on Iona by Norse raiders. Today, tens of thousands of tourists and pilgrims cross the sound of Mull to visit Iona.

By 800AD the Norwegian raiders became settled in the Western Isles, and several of the clans have Norse origins. The clan system was based on the chieftains holding land and attracting followers to protect their interests. Early clan history is rather sparse, although their genealogies often go back into the dark ages. By the second half of the 17th Century, after the decline of the influence of the Clan MacDougal and then Clan MacDonald, who held title over the island, MacLean of Duart was made Baronet by King Robert the Bruce and granted the lands of Mull. A disastrous campaign in the Jacobite cause ended with the battle of Inverkeithing, where Sir Hector Roy MacLean took 800 MacLeans and MacQuarries. Sir Hector was killed and only 35 men returned to Mull. Fortunes fluctuated, but by the end of the 17th Century the chief was in exile and the Duke of Argyll took possession of the island as recompense for accumulated debts.

Many famous visitors came to the island and wrote of their travels. Martin Martin, a native of the Isle of Skye, wrote 'A Description of the Western Islands of Scotland' in 1719. This is a fascinating collection of fact and legend in which he describes the island's features. Boswell and Johnson both wrote books on their travels, and their visit to Mull gives us a good description of life on the island in 1773. Mendelssohn visited Staffa, staying on the way in Tobermory, where he may have written the beginnings of 'Fingal's Cave'.

Anyone who visits Mull cannot fail to be impressed by the sheer variety in the landscape. In the south the mountain masses make a fine backdrop, while Glen More winds its way through the hills to the softer scenery of the Ross of Mull. Calgary beach in the north and Lagain sands (Lochbuie) in the south are two of the finest beaches to be found anywhere in Scotland, whilst the waterfalls and lochs that abound throughout the island are often set off by old woodlands of hazel and birch. It is because of this diversity of habitat that the island is one of the prime places to study wildlife and flora in Britain.

Besides the beauty of the scenery there are legends of the supernatural, headless horsemen, a Kelpie in Loch Scridain, ghostly pipers in MacKinnon's Cave and many others. The island has a strong musical tradition and a music festival is held every year in April. The island is a Mecca for yachtsmen and in West Highland Week a mass of colourful sails is to be seen in the Sound of Mull as the cream of Scottish yachts race in the final leg of the week. In July every year the Mull Highland Games attracts high class competitors and with a large crowd of visitors the games field is a whirl of piping, dancing, throwing events and foot races. To round off the year the Tour of Mull Car Rally takes place in the middle of October, an event that has been a great success for many years now.

I have lived and worked on the Isle of Mull for over 37 years, and a large part of my spare time has been spent walking the hills and glens of the island. Yet I never tire of revisiting favourite walks or going in search of new areas and finding new delights. Many of the favourites such as the Fossil Tree, Carsaig Arches and the Treshnish Headland are among the landscapes depicted in this book.

Bill Clegg, Curator of the Mull Museum in Tobermory
February 2006

The Lismore Light. The lighthouse is on neither Mull nor Iona — but it earns its place in this book on account of how, like clockwork, it looms first to starboard then to port when sailing to and from Mull.

Decommissioned fishing vessels strategically abandoned so that we might ponder their slow return to nature, Salen Bay.

Rotting hull, dyke and shed, near Salen. It seems to be a Hebridean tradition to let old boats die peacefully where they fell.

Standing stone by Tenga, Glen Aros.

Mull & Iona

A gentle-looking ruin perpetually enjoyed from this one viewpoint on the main road North to Tobermory. Gentle-looking it may be, but it was in fact a scene of great treachery in 1608 when Lord Ochiltree, acting as the Kings representative, lured several Highland chiefs onto his ship with a dinner invitation, then clapped them in irons and took them off to Edinburgh.

Mull & Iona

*The broad sweep of the harbour front at Tobermory, here viewed from the working pier
as the town begins to stir on a radiant summer's morning.*

Tobermory back yards, where creels cohabit with laundry. The town is not entirely devoted to children, but it can seem that way!

This is the sight the tourist promoters tend not to promote – but as we all know, it's like this most of the time.

A deep-frozen Tobermory takes on a rosy yuletide glow, Christmas 1995.

A curious enamelled seafaring cherub – once a fountain – seems somehow connected in spirit to the working fleet behind, Tobermory Harbour.

West Street, Tobermory. This street can't conceal its infant appeal. Miss Houlie's Cottage is the green one with the fire in the hearth.

Josie Jump from the BBC TV series Balamory during a shoot on the film set at Tobermory. You can be sure that images of the town are now engraved in the minds of millions of kids worldwide.

Previous page: Tobermory was built as a planned village for workers of the 19th century west coast fishing industry, and its architectural legacy has prevailed to iconic proportions. Here the morning light picks out all the colours and harmonies of this special little world.

Timber bows and seagulls at low tide, Tobermory Harbour.

Tobermory Bay really is as pretty as this.

Tobermory Bay from the cliff top at Beadoun in full summer light.

The texture is changed but the place is unmistakable. Tobermory waterfront in snow.

Ardnamurchan Peninsula kissed by a late splash of warm light behind the Lighthouse at Rhuba nan Gal, Tobermory.

In splendid isolation at the end of a stunning 'c' road stands the impressive Glengorm Castle. A rich Hebridean sunset picks out the Island of Coll on the horizon.

The trio of standing stones at Glengorm. Not all ancient sites feel special, but these stones have a presence – perhaps simply because they were erected in such an exquisite corner of the island.

A moody sky and restless tide on the rocky shore at Glengorm.

The bathing pool, Glengorm.

Excavation has shown that these stones were originally in a straight line. With Coll and the great Atlantic beyond, they still look very much at one with each other.

The Mishnish Lochs on the road to Dervaig. Foreboding cloud and stark rowan set off the rich browns of this early spring scene.

Mull & Iona

The charming village of Dervaig, originally home to the Mull Little Theatre, nestles in a natural glen defined by Loch a Chumhainn and the River Bellart. It is identifiable from all angles by the white pencil tower of the church.

Dervaig Church. The eye is drawn to the bold pencil-shaped tower of this lovingly restored church.

A lone goose silhouetted at Loch Chumhainn, Dervaig. The goose has an easiness about it that suggests a relatively domestic lifestyle.

Edge of the dunes, Calgary beach. This beach is highly revered by those looking for the real Hebridean beach experience — and for good reason. The quality of its sand is quite sumptuous.

Calgary Bay. An Irish-style shack, roofing by virtue of an upturned wooden dinghy. On closer inspection it appears to be used for serving tea to visitors.

Calgary Bay. Understandably a place of pilgrimage for our North American cousins, the bay delivers real pristine beauty.

Approaching Calgary Bay from the Dervaig Road.

Calgary Bay. A gloriously climactic west coast sunset hits its peak as a freshwater burn gently meanders before delivering itself to the sea.

An invigorating walk to Treshnish Point rewards with intimate views of great spume-filled seas crashing on defiant igneous rock features such as Dun Haum, which was once an Iron Age Fort.

On the cliff top above Dun Haun, the Treshnish Isles shimmer in the fleeting spring light.

Crakaig is idyllically located in its own little world. This pre-clearance village is wonderfully evocative of the chosen lifestyle these hardy island dwellers once enjoyed/ endured. It is easy to feel romantic about that era in places like this.

Rhuidle, by Treshnish. A sturdy remnant of an abandoned township.

Highland cattle on the west coast of Mull, looking to Ben More from Ballygown.

Dutchman's Cap fits this west coast Highlander perfectly.

Cottage at Kilbrennan. Loch Tuath with Ulva and Gribun can be seen in the distance.

Ben More resplendent in stunning winter light, offset by a pair of unmatched blackface ewes. Kilninian, Loch Tuath.

Waterfall by Ballygown, west coast.

Sugar-pink sunlight kisses the summit of Ben More – a good moment for a sundowner. Ulva Ferry.

Dinghy moorings at Ulva Ferry.

A Blackface tup ruminates contentedly among the machair, Ulva.

These sheep make chilling out look so easy! Loch na Keal and Island of Eorsa, early morning.

Spring sunlight creates heavenly shafts of pure blue light that occasionally burst through the fleeting clouds dancing among the Ben More range across Loch na Keal.

Crystal clear views across Eorsa and Loch na Keal to the Ben More range.

Translucent early light enhances the tranquility of Loch na Keal and Eorsa with Gribun in the distance.

Pedigree beef cattle laze contentedly around the shores of Loch Ba, an impressive stretch of water noted for its salmon fishing and once the location of the caldera in geological history.

A descent from Ben More to just beneath the cloud cover. The day subsides across Ulva and Eorsa, ruby red in classic west coast fashion.

The raised beach along this inspiring road delivers a topography of great texture. Meanwhile, cloud shifts rapidly across the great rock mass of Gribun – bringing the promise of a rich sunset.

Mull & Iona

A magical moment on the tortuous and dramatic road from Salen to Gribun: a rainbow clings to the severe basalt slopes.

A glistening road to Gribun, blinding with reflections from a setting sun – which promises a spectacular sunset up Loch na Keal.

A rich tapestry of dusky colours evolves swiftly in the sky above Eorsa and Gribun as the day subsides into the Western Ocean.

An engaging vernacular-style dwelling (the original Granny's Heeland Hame perhaps?)
nestles beneath the high corries above Balnahard, Gribun.

Balmeanach Farm and a view to the west from the steep ascent up the hill from Gribun.

Three red deer hinds at Burg. The arduous trek from Tiroran to the wilderness on the edge of the Ardmeanach Peninsula afforded this surprise encounter.

A joy to behold: lazy fronds of kelp luxuriate in the crystal-clear tidal shorelines of a pristine stretch of coast at Ardmeanach.

Burg Shore. Straps of glistening kelp tossed by nature across a saddle of rock – a lovely sight to sustain the walker on pilgrimage to the Fossil Tree.

The Fossil Tree itself is a visual non-event, but this is a sublime piece of shoreline where treasure is all around, such as these strands of kelp and shiny wet basalt pebbles.

A cave at the Wilderness Beach by the Fossil Tree. The stones look sensual – but they do rattle and squeak as you stumble about this gem of a place.

Looking across Loch Scridain to Ardmeanach from Aird Fada.

Somehow the scale of the geology at the Burg is augmented by modest buildings such as these at Ardtun and Achnahard.

Bunessan is a focal point for the communities of the Ross of Mull. The village nestles around a tidal bay in Loch na Lathaich.

Heading westwards, the Ross of Mull opens up with broad vistas to the north – as at this point just past Bunessan.

Mull & Iona

Fionnphort beach. Working creels impose on the foreground in front of the split rock that is forever perched in the centre of this delightful beach.

The Bull Hole in winter, Fionnphort. This is a sheltered passage where commercial boats – and even the Iona ferry – go to hide from the fresh conditions often found in the Sound of Iona

Fionnphort in the snow of 1995. Columba, a wee boat, Iona Abbey in the distance – a curious symbolism is suggested by this particular rotting hull.

Iona

The translucent waters of St Ronan's Bay.

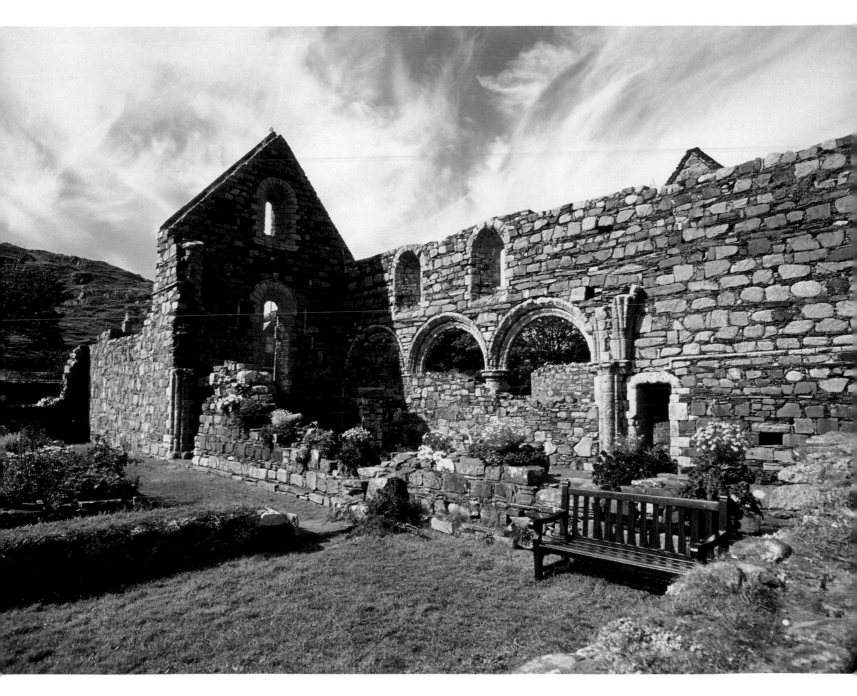

The gracefully weathered masonry of Iona's Nunnery encloses the tranquil atmosphere created within the ruin.

The Abbey is visited by tens of thousands of visitors each year, and is a primary focus for Christian pilgrimages. The pilgrims pay homage to the work of St Columba, who first converted the Scots to Christianity in AD563.

The Cloisters, Iona Abbey.

Mull & Iona

North End beach, or Traigh Ban, is a beach of exquisite beauty – viewed here in its most vibrant summer plumage.

The White Strand of the Monks. Monks might once have walked here in prayer, while still keeping sight of the Abbey to the south.

The northern beaches offer quintessential Hebridean beauty, and seas that emanate pure joy. The island of Mull lies just on the near horizon.

Mull & Iona

Looking down the Sound of Iona from the pier.

Overleaf: *Camas Bay is also known as 'the beach at the back of the ocean'. The pink sand and green machair together create a slice of natural paradise.*

Camas Bay at the end of a perfect day. Another face of this stunning beach.

Columba's Bay, where it is believed St Columba landed from Ireland. It is a fair trek from the Abbey, but nevertheless pilgrimages will descend out of nowhere upon this place throughout the year.

Port na Curaich, or 'Bay of the Coracle'. Glorious summer sun sparkles off the blue waters at the south end of the island.

Mull & Iona

The beach at Traigh Mhor, Sound of Iona. The clarity of the waters around Iona's shore have become something of a legend.

MacDonald's boat, reassuringly beached in its own wee bay. Somehow only Iona can generate images of this purity.

One of the working inshore boats that are often moored in St Ronan's Bay.

The shore at Baile Mor, Iona village. There is Hebridean easiness about the way the gardens on the front merge with the foreshore. Boundaries, it seems, are not important here.

Like a page from a Katie Morag story, the part-faded, part-cherished setting for Iona's post office is very engaging to see.

Dunsmeorach, former residence of George MacLeod, founder of the Iona Community.

Dawn breaks across the bay at Baile Mor to the grating call of a stray corncrake taking refuge in the Abbey gardens.

In the grip of winter.

The Abbey, beautiful in the singular ambience of this wintry day.

We now leave Iona and return to Mull.

A rainbow blesses the holy Island of Iona. View across the Sound of Iona from Port Mor on the very western most tip of the Ross of Mull.

Nature's designs can be rich, complex and beautiful – like this sky and lush textural shoreline at Fidden, most westerly end of the Ross.

Crystal-clear aquamarine waters lap the pristine shore of Ardalanish Bay.

Mull & Iona

The shore near Carsaig, looking west.

The shore from Carsaig to the Arches is strewn with fascinating natural objets d'art such as this boulder, perhaps a volcanic bomb.

The gentle ebb and flow of the tide in the rock pools create kelp-like, lyrical shapes.

A comic pose from a magnificent feral goat on the Carsaig Arches coastal trail.

Up close, the Carsaig Arches are quite awesome – rather like some ancient steam-powered fantasy warship.

Carsaig - Loch Buie Trail. Waterfall and sheep skeleton.

"This is a old boat. It sounded like this BANG CRASH when it was on the sea. It broke on a big Rock." By Amber, age 6 (at Pennyghael).

Arriving in Lochbuie is an experience in itself, producing a great sense of deliverance as the road is long and very rough – not for the faint-hearted. This may explain why the place is such a treasure, possessing an atmosphere of solitude and timelessness.

Mull & Iona

Lochbuie in one of its more brooding moments, Lochbuie House and Moy Castle.

Lagian Sands, Lochbuie.

Mull & Iona

This stone is a singular outlier from the nearby Lochbuie Stone Circle.

Moy Castle stands in one of those locations that is so evocative you couldn't dream it up.

Lochbuie House, austere and imposing, presides quietly on the shore beneath Creach Beinn.

Mull & Iona

An Leárg, Lochbuie. Thankfully, Mull still possesses bits of good old-fashioned Hebridean tumbledown. These places often become sheilings for feral-looking herds of hill cattle.

Lochdon – another of Mull's many facets – evokes a sheltered and fertile feel.

The herd of easy-going Highlanders that inhabit the environs of Duart Castle are at ease with the camera. They have done this before!

Duart Castle and the Mull ferry against the backdrop of Ardnamurchan. All three elements fuse with breathtaking clarity on this rare winter's day.

Mull & Iona

A stunning west highland castle, Duart, stronghold of the MacLeans, stands easy and proud across the Sound of Mull. The castle was purchased and restored at the beginning of last century by Colonel Sir Fitzroy Donald MacLean.

*An explosion of intense yellow light bursts out from behind the distant Cruachan hills
– drama that only Duart Castle could possibly match.*

Twa calves, Duart.

Duart from Torosay. Isn't it great the way cattle randomly fire off a darn good moo-ing when the moment takes them?

Torosay Castle and gardens. A lush and sophisticated garden of great elegance is presided over by the baronial towers of the castle.

Torosay garden. Subtle details such as this confirm the care that has been bestowed on this charming place.

Verdant growth characterises the influence of the Gulf Stream on these flowers in Torosay gardens.

The Camellias and the steps at Torosay Castle. Such dignified splendour takes time to cultivate.